First World War
and Army of Occupation
War Diary
France, Belgium and Germany

23 DIVISION
Divisional Troops
Royal Army Medical Corps
Divisional Field Ambulance Workshop Unit
30 July 1915 - 31 March 1916

WO95/2180/1

The Naval & Military Press Ltd
www.nmarchive.com
Published in association with The National Archives

Published by

The Naval & Military Press Ltd

Unit 10 Ridgewood Industrial Park,

Uckfield, East Sussex,

TN22 5QE England

Tel: +44 (0) 1825 749494

www.naval-military-press.com

www.nmarchive.com

This diary has been reprinted in facsimile from the original. Any imperfections are inevitably reproduced and the quality may fall short of modern type and cartographic standards.

© **Crown Copyright**
Images reproduced by permission of The National Archives, London, England, 2015.

Contents

Document type	Place/Title	Date From	Date To
Heading	WO95/2180/1 23 Divn-Divnl Troops Divnl Field Ambulance Workshop Unit 1915 July-1916 March		
Heading	23rd Division 23rd Divl Fd Amb W" Shop Unit Jly 1915-Mar 1916		
Heading	23rd Division 23rd Divl F.A. Workshop Unit Vol I July Aug Sept 15		
Heading	War Diary Of 23rd Divl Field Ambulance Workshop Unit From 30th July 1915 To 30th September 1915		
War Diary	Grovepark	30/07/1915	30/07/1915
War Diary	Staines	31/07/1915	31/07/1915
War Diary	Bulford	31/07/1915	23/08/1915
War Diary	Avonmouth	24/08/1915	25/08/1915
War Diary	Southampton	25/08/1915	25/08/1915
War Diary	Havre	26/08/1915	26/08/1915
War Diary	Rouen	28/08/1915	29/08/1915
War Diary	Abbeville	30/08/1915	30/08/1915
War Diary	Moringhem	31/08/1915	03/09/1915
War Diary	La Communal	04/09/1915	06/09/1915
War Diary	Wallon Cappel	07/09/1915	07/09/1915
War Diary	Vieux Berquin	08/09/1915	15/09/1915
War Diary	La Menegate	16/09/1915	30/09/1915
Heading	23rd Division 23rd F.A. W.U. Vol 2 Oct 15		
Heading	War Diary Of 23rd Field Ambulance Workshop Unit From 1st-31st Oct. 1915		
War Diary	Lamenegate	01/10/1915	31/10/1915
Heading	23rd Division 23rd F.A W.U. Vol.3 Nov.15		
Heading	War Diary Of 23rd Field Ambulance Workshop Unit From 1st-30th Nov. 1915		
War Diary	La Menegate	01/11/1915	30/11/1915
Heading	23rd F.A. W.U. Vol 4 Dec 1915 121/7931		
Heading	War Diary Of 23rd Div. Field Ambulance Workshop Unit From 1st-31st Dec 1915		
War Diary	Lamenegate	01/12/1915	31/12/1915
Heading	23rd F.A. W.U. Vol. 5 January 1916		
War Diary	Lamenegate	01/01/1916	13/01/1916
Heading	War Diary Of 23rd Div. Field Ambulance & Workshop Unit From 1st-To 31st January 1916		
War Diary	Lamenegate	14/01/1916	31/01/1916
Heading	War Diaries Of 23rd Divisional Field Ambulance Workshop Units A.S.C. For The Months Of February And March 1916		
Heading	War Diary Of 23rd Div F.A. & W.U. From 1st Feby To 29 Febry 1916 23 F.A.W.U. Vol.6		
War Diary	La Menegate	01/02/1916	21/02/1916
War Diary	Morbecques	22/02/1916	29/02/1916
Heading	War Diary Of 23rd Div. F.A. & W.U. From 1st-31st March 1916 23 F.a. W.U. Vol. 7		
War Diary	Bruay	01/03/1916	22/03/1916
War Diary	Barlin	22/03/1916	31/03/1916

WO 95 2180/1

23 Divn - Divnl Troops

DIVNL FIELD AMBULANCE WORKSHOP VISIT

1915 JULY - 1916 MARCH

23RD DIVISION

23RD DIVL FD AMB W'SHOP UNIT

JLY 1915 - MAR 1916

23rd Khirwin

23rd Div: F.A. workshops Unit
Vol. I
July, Aug & Sept 15

Jly '15
Mar '16

Confidential

War Diary

of

23rd Divl Field Ambulance "Workshop" Unit

from 30th July 1915 to 30th September 1915

P Baylor 2/Lieut, A.S.C.
Commanding 23rd Div. F.A. & W.U.

WAR DIARY
or
INTELLIGENCE SUMMARY
(Erase heading not required.)

Army Form C.2118

Place	Date 1915	Hour	Summary of Events and Information	Remarks and references to Appendices
GROVE PARK	30/7/15	3.15pm	Left GROVE PARK with cars. Personnel complete. Reached STAINES 6 p.m.	
STAINES	31/7/15	9am	Left STAINES for BULFORD arrived 7 p.m. Two Daimlers with (worn) gearshafts.	
BULFORD	31/7/15 to 8/8/15 to 22/8/15		At BULFORD training men - obtaining new men in place of insufficients - those who declined to be inoculated - repairing damaged gear shaft, completing equipment.	
BULFORD	23/8/15	7am	Left BULFORD for Avonmouth - arrived 5 p.m. without incident	
AVONMOUTH	24/8/15		AVONMOUTH - Loaded cars on board two transports with some men in charge in each ship	
AVONMOUTH	25/8/15	10.10 a.m.	Entrained with remaining 59 men for SOUTHAMPTON - arrived 1.30 p.m. Entrained on S.S. "Queen Alexandra" 5 p.m.	
SOUTHAMPTON	8/15	7pm	Left for HAVRE - arrived without incident 1.30 a.m. Ship very crowded.	
HAVRE	26/8/15	6am	Left for ROUEN - arrived that about 2 p.m. Marched men to rest camp	
ROUEN	28/8/15		Remained at ROUEN - completed details of new equipment - pass new cars arrived.	
	29/8/15		Left for Abbeville ABBEVILLE arrived 6 p.m. towing one car with broken radiator - Endeavoured unsuccessfully to obtain a second radiator. Left car at Base for repair	

WAR DIARY or INTELLIGENCE SUMMARY

Army Form C. 2118

Place	Date	Hour	Summary of Events and Information	Remarks and references to Appendices
ABBEVILLE	30/8/15	9 am	Left for Tilques. TILQUES & reported at Hqrs 23rd Div. at 5 p.m. ordered to divide into 3 sections — send one to MORINGHEM — one to LOSTRAT + one to MOULLE — No 1 Section with horses arrived at MORINGHEM at 9 p.m. Joined 69th Fld. Amb.	
MORINGHEM	8/31/15		Visited other 2 sections at LOSTRAT + MOULLE later inspected route for General's inspection on 1st Sep	
	2/9/15	6 am	General's inspection — cars taken over stubble field, no roads closed	
	3/9/15		Three with Fld Ambulance to La Communal.	
	4/9/15		Repairing car with damaged gears (Daimler) many isolated calls for sick patients to be moved in motor ambulances.	
WALLON CAPPEL	6/9/15	6 am	Left for WALLON CAPPEL with whole division — Very many fell out from each Brigade — arrived 5 p.m. very hot.	
	7/9/15	9 am	Left for VIEUX BERQUIN arrived about 4 p.m.	
VIEUX BERQUIN	8/9/15		Visited other sections at OULTERSTEENE and BAILLEUL inspected camp	
	9/9/15		do	do

WAR DIARY or INTELLIGENCE SUMMARY

Army Form C. 2118

Place	Date	Hour	Summary of Events and Information	Remarks and references to Appendices
Vieux Berquin	10/9/15		VIEUX BERQUIN - Cars employed twenty with Sick Cases 8 K.O.Y.L.I. & 11th W. Ridings	
do	11/9/15		do	
	12/9/15		Visited AIRE to interview D.D.M.S. I.C. reported all arrangements carried out in the working of Field Ambulances - instructed to report any case of difficulty.	
d.	13/9/15		Daily visit to other sections - Cars fairly well employed.	
d.	14/9/15		do	
d.	15/9/15		do	
LA MENEGATE	16/9/15		Left VIEUX BERQUIN for LA MENEGATE Found other sections within few miles.	
d.	17/9/15		Cars early in use for Casual wounded from trenches -	
do	18/9/15		Some cars sent to Advanced Dressing Stations BOIS GRENIER & GRIS POT	
do	19/9/15		do still at do	
do	20/9/15		do also at PORT ROMPU dressing station, other sections visited daily	
			at ERQUINGHEM ESTRADE & STEENWERCK	
d.	21/9/15		Cars fairly fully employed - Received orders from D.D.M.S. I.C. to add 2 lorries	
d.	24/9/15		& 6 cars to move and do my own for Marine. Shelling of German aeroplanes overhead. Shrapnel bullets struck my car & one employed Shell just flung past.	
do	25/9/15		Very heavy bombardment. Many wounded. Many wounded dealt with - (are doing good work S Two Bearer Coll(s) + Van Battn with A.D./D.S.S./Forms/C. 2118. bad sound. The cars worked on	

WAR DIARY
or
INTELLIGENCE SUMMARY

Army Form C. 2118

Place	Date	Hour	Summary of Events and Information	Remarks and references to Appendices
LAMERGATE	26/9/15		Cars busy with wounded. 66h & 70h 2nd Ambulances. 71st at Hospital is busy with wounded.	
do.	27/9/15		Few wounded. Staff with the cars finishing repairs. Second nearly finished - now running well. Relieved Div Sanitary lorry from a ditch.	
do	28/9/15		Few wounded - usual daily inspection - motored 2 Section sergts to be more careful in seeing that drivers attend to cars underneath. Big guns again beginning tonight. Germans nervous - judging by their star shells - 4 Prisoners seen today, looks very badly wounded but relieved at being captured.	
do	29/9/15		Very heavy rain - roads very bad - ? why roads from ARMENTIERES to SAILLY & MERVILLE not made up at sides of pavé - feet of mud - roads very much used by all branches. French authorities very busily employed mending much less important roads.	
do	30/9/15		Careful detailed inspection of all cars. Daimlers standing up to the work better than anticipated, but fear gears will become more numerous as weaker troubles get worse - Gear box not a suitable type for the rough driving class of driver - Can be much damaged by one or two careless changes in a few minutes - Frames appear well up to the work as now strengthened - Springing good - Bodywork satisfactory with few modifications now made giving better access to underpart of chassis. Attachment of dashboards defective. Paintwork much too conspicuous & being altered - as soon as paint can be obtained some observers are made much too dark - a medium green blue appears to be most suitable in this country. Ford cars appear to stand up very well as regards	

Place	Date	Hour	Summary of Events and Information	Remarks and references to Appendices
Lamersgelt	30/9/15		engine "chassis" - but bodywork very poor - It has apparently been found that four stretcher cases are too great a load as instructions have been received to do away with top tier leaving only two stretcher cases on floor of body. A means of access (for 3 sitting cases) from the front is highly desirable but the alterations entailed are rather too extensive to be tackled by two carpenters when the cars are in heavy work & cannot be spared for any length of time - Have received instructions not to attempt such reconstruction of bodywork for that reason — Some possible difficulty was anticipated with regard to the control to be taken of the Ambulance Cars & the A.S.C. drivers, but discussion of the points involved with the C.O.'s of the three Field Ambulances have prevented any such difficulties materializing — A respectful protest against the unauthorised driving of the cars was fully entered by the C.O. of the Field Ambulance concerned. Pointing out the difficulty involved in bringing home to the drivers any careless handling of their cars should good ground for the protest. The awful "granite" with which the roads are mended - never apparently rolled in — causes much damage to tyres	

J. Bayley
LIEUT, A.S.C.
COMMANDING 23rd DIV. F.A. & W.U.

121/7517

2nd Division

23rd F.A. W.U.
Vol 2
Oct. 15

Oct. 1915

Confidential.

War Diary
— of —

23rd Div. Field Ambulance "Workshop Unit

From 1st — 31st Oct: 1915

J.S. Ayley
LIEUT, A.S.C. M.T.
COMMANDING 23RD DIV. F.A. & W.U.

Army Form C. 2118

WAR DIARY
or
INTELLIGENCE SUMMARY
(Erase heading not required.)

Instructions regarding War Diaries and Intelligence Summaries are contained in F.S. Regs., Part II. and the Staff Manual respectively. Title Pages will be prepared in manuscript.

FIELD AMBULANCE AND WORKSHOP UNIT — 23rd DIV

Place	Date	Hour	Summary of Events and Information	Remarks and references to Appendices
MENEGATE	1/10/15		Usual daily inspection:— Floorboards of Ambulance bodies being gradually altered so cars can be brought in from service:—	
do	2/10/15		Daily inspection:— Men appear to be paying careful attention to the necessity for keeping all nuts tight — Daimler engines have serious risk of loosening rear engine bolts— most particularly on right side (when facing engine) The drivers reported today that bolt required tightening after each run — (Engine to be tuned up).	
do	3/10/15		Daily inspection	
do	4/10/15		do.	
do	5/10/15		do.	
do	6/10/15		do.	
do	7/10/15		do. cars not having a regular routine of running — men find it rather difficult to keep records of chassis continuously clean:— Rule made that underneath must be cleaned at least once a day thoroughly — at most convenient free time — as a regular hour appears impossible:—	
do	8/10/15		Daily inspection.	
do	9/10/15		do.— A.D.Med. wishes & inspects Workshops 10.20 pm. Snipes at when returning from Mess of 69 F.A.	
do	10/10/15		do.— Reports sniping to A.P.M. Requested to act as being again bright with searchlamp. 9 pm dil	

Army Form C. 2118

WAR DIARY
or
INTELLIGENCE SUMMARY
(Erase heading not required.)

Instructions regarding War Diaries and Intelligence Summaries are contained in F.S. Regs., Part II. and the Staff Manual respectively. Title Pages will be prepared in manuscript.

Place	Date	Hour	Summary of Events and Information	Remarks and references to Appendices
La MENEGATE	11/10/15		Daily Inspection. Divns attached to 71st Field Ambulance appear to suffer more from sickness than any of the others. They are better housed, well fed & have at present less	
	12/10/15	3.45	MOR saw either of the four sections - got each case of minor sickness - yet more sickness have recurred amongst them - Ordered by APM to report at once any further suspicious event in district. Inspection by General Babington - Commanding 23rd Division - Everything correct & the General was of opinion that my Unit should be very comfortable at Ferme Dechief :-	
	13/10/15		Daily inspection - Continuing general First overhaul of all cars:-	
	14/10/15		do	do
	15/10/15		do	do Two wounded "sick"
	16/10/15		do	do do
	17/10/15		do	do do
	18/10/15		do	do do
	19/10/15		do. German aeroplane passed over here "dropped a coloured streamer (weighted) which dropped about 100 yards behind our Ferme. Recovered same & reported at once to Div. Hdqrs who handed over streamer. Apparently it was fact that sheds near where two 9" big guns are situated - Div Hdqrs stated that	

1875 Wt. W593/826 1,000,000 4/15 J.B.C. & A. A.D.S.S./Forms/C.2118.

WAR DIARY or INTELLIGENCE SUMMARY

Army Form C. 2118

Instructions regarding War Diaries and Intelligence Summaries are contained in F.S. Regs., Part II. and the Staff Manual respectively. Title Pages will be prepared in manuscript.

(Erase heading not required.)

Place	Date	Hour	Summary of Events and Information	Remarks and references to Appendices
LA MENEGATE	19/10/15		"Gunners would be warned at once". — Men moved into Barn the Winter Quarters	
	20/10/15		Inspection. Two wounded. — Continuing overhaul of cars.	
	21/10/15		do. do. Frames Spring of Daimler ambulances shewing weakness of front dump irons — Am plugging same with hard wood in channel - this highly hooked right through will two bolts to stiffen	
	22/10/15		Ordinary Routine - one or two drivers not so careful of cleaning as they might be.	
	23/10/15		Reports to S.D. & T. AIRE "All correct" - Inspection —	
	24/10/15		Inspection. Two wounded. Men very comfortable in barn	
	25/10/15		do. Continuing car overhauls.	
	26/10/15		do. do. Learnt that practically all men stated by me from hqrs 70th Field Ambulance for admission to A/O have been ordered to join up at Rouen immediately. — Allowed to by R.A.M.C. Officers that A.S.C. were recruiting at R.A.M.C's expense. I pointed out that however (most of them) would be more usefully employed in A.S.C. — That our R.A.M.C. men could be trained in a week or two for stretcher duties — but that it took a long time to properly train an A.S.C. driver or mechanic	
	27/10/15		Inspection — Roads very bad — much rain	
	28/10/15		do. much more rain	

WAR DIARY
or
INTELLIGENCE SUMMARY
(Erase heading not required.)

Army Form C. 2118

Place	Date	Hour	Summary of Events and Information	Remarks and references to Appendices
LAMENEGATE	29/10/15		Inspection:- Roads getting worse.	
	30/10/15		Inspection:- Reported to D.D.S.T at AIRE. Have found that the high dashboard of the Daimlers has become very loose on many of the cars owing to its being insufficiently stayed. Am fitting strong forged brackets direct to frame of chassis which stiffens them very considerably.	
	31/10/15		Inspection- Water tubes- Further general overhaul of cars suspended for hire being owing to possible urgent use for hire. After a further month of ordinary usage without any great pause, all the cars would appear to be standing up well to the work, considering the condition of the roads. Drivers are handling their Daimlers much better as a result of careful coaching - All have been severely warned as to the consequences of driving beyond the regulation pace at any time - All my Ford cars have had their upper shields running removed & they are standing up well. Tyre wear is rather heavy in all cases - the large sharp flints frequently causing severe gashes in the covers - A number on hand for repair as torn as to allow canvas can be renewed. A goodly number of covers would appear to be "old stock" M'defective manufacture as in many cases the tread has separated very readily from the canvas, from no apparent reason.	

P. Gayley
LIEUT. A.S.C. M.T.
COMMANDING 23RD DIV. F.A. & W.U.

23rd 2.a.W.O.
Vol. 3

F/7635

23 Feb Werin

Nov 15

F

Nov. 1915

Confidential

War Diary

of

23rd Field Ambulance Workshop Unit

From 1st — 30th Nov. 1915

H Gayler 2/Lieut, A.S.C.
Commanding 23rd Div. F.A. & W.U.

Army Form C. 2118

WAR DIARY
or
INTELLIGENCE SUMMARY
(Erase heading not required.)

Instructions regarding War Diaries and Intelligence Summaries are contained in F.S. Regs., Part II. and the Staff Manual respectively. Title Pages will be prepared in manuscript.

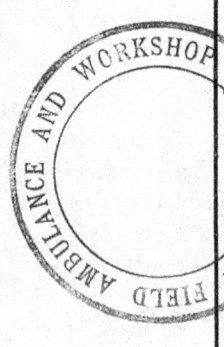

Place	Date	Hour	Summary of Events and Information	Remarks and references to Appendices
LA MIENIEGATE	1/11/15		Daily inspection - Weather very bad.	
	2/11/15		do. slippery	
	3/11/15		do. - much rain - roads awful	
	4/11/15		do. - do	
	5/11/15		do. - finer but showery.	
	6/11/15		Reports to D.D.S.T. AIRE - Very much better but no rain - daily inspection	
	7/11/15		Daily inspection - wet & muddy - very difficult to keep cars clean. No supplies of waste & cleaning rags much delayed.	
	8/11/15		Daily inspection —	
	9/11/15		do - GRIS POT. Attacked # dressing station of 69th F.A. heavily shelled. One of my drivers severely wounded by piece of H.E. shell - perforated lung - House in which A.D.S. installed shelled & collapsed on the top of one of the Ford Ambulances - Succeeded after

1875 Wt. W593/826 1,000,000 4/15 J.B.C. & A. A.D.S.S./Forms/C.2118.

WAR DIARY
or
INTELLIGENCE SUMMARY
(Erase heading not required.)

Army Form C. 2118

Instructions regarding War Diaries and Intelligence Summaries are contained in F.S. Regs., Part II. and the Staff Manual respectively. Title Pages will be prepared in manuscript.

Place	Date	Hour	Summary of Events and Information	Remarks and references to Appendices
LAMENEGHE	10/11/15		death in dressing car — getting same down to FORT ROMPU with own power. Driver Griffiths taken to hospital by 26th F.A. very serious condition	
	11/11/15		Visited Griffiths in Hospital — Case hopeless — Brought Car to Workshop under own power — Body crushed — nearly perforated by piece of shell + hawthorn bushes — starboard rear spring broken — Griffiths died at 1 pm today — twice at EROUINGHEM. He had been very plucky, before he was wounded ("volunteered") to fetch dressings for wounded men (as officer) although shelling still continued. Daily inspection — Informed by A.D.M.S. that Griffiths has been recommended for D.C.M. Wrote his wife three times to break it gently to her as am FOS. She is an invalid. — Purchased material for repair of Ford. Commenced warm tyres/comforts — This case comforts received from —	
	12/11/15		Daily inspection — This case comforts received from — Repairs to smashed Fords are proceeding ment very pleased.	
	13/11/15		Daily Inspection visited AIRE to report to MERVILLE but tried without success to find LAHORE Field Ambulance to inspect instead of dog biting	

1875 Wt. W593/826 1,000,000 4/15 J.B.C. & A. A.D.S.S./Forms/C.2118.

Army Form C.2118

WAR DIARY
or
INTELLIGENCE SUMMARY
(Erase heading not required.)

Instructions regarding War Diaries and Intelligence Summaries are contained in F.S. Regs., Part II. and the Staff Manual respectively. Title Pages will be prepared in manuscript.

Place	Date	Hour	Summary of Events and Information	Remarks and references to Appendices
LA MENEGATE	14/11/15		for use near trenches at night.	
	15/11/15		Slight frost last night. Learnt today that no glycerine at all available for anti freezing mixtures. Imperative to procure methylated spirit in lieu — Found some at LA GORGUES — Delivered 5 gall drum to each section with clear instructions as to use. Labor F.A. formerly at LA GORGUES left routine & swore for the South — Decided to improvise lighting accumulated	
	16/11/15		Daily inspection — Very heavy frost night of 14/15 — found no radiator or engine jackets suffered — Intimate that methylated was served out yesterday.	
	17/11/15		Daily inspection — Heavy frosts continue.	
	18/11/15		do.	
	19/11/15		do.	
	20/11/15		do. Methylated solution effective.	
	21/11/15		do. Reported to O.C. S. & T. at AIRES.	
	22/11/15		Daily inspection — Heavy night frosts — thawing rapidly during day — Instructed Section Sergeants to broken up methylated solution in radiators	
			Daily inspection. Frost held all day today	

Army Form C.2118

WAR DIARY
or
INTELLIGENCE SUMMARY
(Erase heading not required.)

Instructions regarding War Diaries and Intelligence Summaries are contained in F. S. Regs., Part II. and the Staff Manual respectively. Title Pages will be prepared in manuscript.

Place	Date	Hour	Summary of Events and Information	Remarks and references to Appendices
LA MENEGATE	23/11/15		Daily inspection – Frost last last night – roads very bad "types suffering" badly through many large patches of flint now to repair roads :–	
	24/11/15		D. Inspection – Continuing general overhaul of cars – strengthening frames "Hotchkiss"	
	25/11/15		D. Inspection. First men went on leave today. Special circumstances have been informed that for leave purposes this Unit is to be considered with Field Ambulances. As the places allotted average one per day for a total of 500 men – my men are rather fortunate – Provided but that they had only been out here a few months would in good conditions that perhaps they had not much right to expect any favourable consideration for some time, but that doubtless numbers would be altered later on.	
	26/11/15		D. Inspection	
	27/11/15		do. Report(s) of Cars' mileages to point out hours of time & cost involved in such a long journey every week – was informed that returns could be sent by D.R.L.S. If nothing special to report Very hard frost – Radiator of one car slightly frozen in spite of 30% Methylated – No damage :–	

1875 Wt. W593/826 1,000,000 4/15 J.B.C. & A. A.D.S.S./Forms/C. 2118.

WAR DIARY
or
INTELLIGENCE SUMMARY
(Erase heading not required.)

Army Form C. 2118

Instructions regarding War Diaries and Intelligence Summaries are contained in F.S. Regs., Part II. and the Staff Manual respectively. Title Pages will be prepared in manuscript.

Place	Date	Hour	Summary of Events and Information	Remarks and references to Appendices
LA MENEGATE	29/11/15		Daily Inspection. Very hard frost continued - Very difficult to clean cars with much frozen on hard.	
	30/11/15		Daily inspection - Frost broke generally this morning - This caro have suffered no damage therefrom - Roads very bad & "sloppy" - Rotter mud & colder still later. One Daimler fogged - borrowed about 30 mins & (her) & put it! During the month the cars have been kept well employed, especially No. 3 Section with 71 F. Amb. Dealing with Rest Station & Evacuation Hospital. Nos 1. & 2. still employed in routine duties - not a great many wounded but good number Sick :- Cars generally holding up well - but very difficult to keep satisfactorily clean - owing to lack of proper cleaning tools which are very slow in coming forward. Alterations carried out to floors of cars enabling to whole to be removed facilitates undir chassis cleaning. Men have to extemporise cleaning brushes to.	

P. Bayley
LIEUT, A.S.C.
COMMANDING 23rd DIV. F.A. & M.U.

23rd F.A.W.V.
Vol: 4

121/7931

Aug 3

Dec. 1915

Confidential

War Diary

of

23rd Bris. Field Ambulance Workshop Unit

June 1st – 31st Dec 1915

J. Bayley
LIEUT, A.S.C.
COMMANDING 23RD DIV. F.A. & W.U.

Army Form C. 2118

WAR DIARY
or
INTELLIGENCE SUMMARY
(Erase heading not required.)

Instructions regarding War Diaries and Intelligence Summaries are contained in F. S. Regs., Part II. and the Staff Manual respectively. Title Pages will be prepared in manuscript.

23rd DIV FIELD AMBULANCE AND WORKSHOP UNIT

Place	Date	Hour	Summary of Events and Information	Remarks and references to Appendices
LA MENEGATE	1.12/15		Daily Inspection - Very heavy rain - roads very heavy after heavy frost of Sunday + heavy fall:-	
	2.12/15		Daily Inspection - The 2nd for repair - collision - axle cracked - &c.	
	3.12/15		do. Roads very bad :- 2w finished - plated axle.	
	4.12/15		do. Visit to Aire to report - Raining hard :-	
	5.12/15		do. Rain	
	6.12/15		do. do.	
	7.12/15		do. do. have more or less mud very bad	
	8.12/15		do. Approach to my farm getting flooded. Authorities seem to do nothing towards clearing Ditches that River over its banks.	
	9.12/15		Daily Inspection. roads getting worse. 12 inches water for 100 yards near farm.	
	10.12/15		Maybe very tiny - water draining - men keep very well however with amateur doctors	

WAR DIARY
or
INTELLIGENCE SUMMARY

(Erase heading not required.)

Army Form C. 2118

Place	Date	Hour	Summary of Events and Information	Remarks and references to Appendices
LA MENEGATE	11/12/15		Daily inspection. Raining hard – Difficulty in getting my car through the mud – still raining tonight. Shall not be able to go on car tomorrow – must wait through to recent situation & borrow an Ambulance.	
	12/12/15		Water fell during night 4 inches – just got out with car.	
	13/12/15		Water still falling – Daily inspection	
	14/12/15		Daily inspection – "Ford" in ditch message came in – Went on car with lorry – found Ford in 5ft water on its side & must Monde 18 inches by wading managed to attach towing cable & run pulled her out. Engine full of water as widely submerged – towed back to Workshop by 4.30 p.m. – Got 2nd running out again by 7 p.m. Instructions received from A.D.S+T. to transfer my Sunbeam to HQ XV Corps in exchange for Wolseley Aroneghi tender to tomorrow – Several 5.9 G shells fell near 10 ft. our my little damage	
	16/12/15		NARRENT - FONTES to transfer car – General Peck's Jones Jones getting most of bargain as Wolseley had been running 14 months	

Army Form C. 2118

WAR DIARY
or
INTELLIGENCE SUMMARY
(Erase heading not required.)

Instructions regarding War Diaries and Intelligence Summaries are contained in F. S. Regs., Part II. and the Staff Manual respectively. Title Pages will be prepared in manuscript.

Place	Date	Hour	Summary of Events and Information	Remarks and references to Appendices
LA MENEGATE	16/12/15		Found Wolseley lorry (C) "traffized". According to her history not yet overhauled.	
	17/12/15		Daily inspection – Saunders 1st speed gears giving trouble.	
	18/12/15		Telegraphic orders from D.A.D.T. to take over Foden steam lorry for 71st F.A. at AIRE – Left my driver to act as guide – Foden arrived safely at 8 pm.	
	19/12/15		Daily Inspection – Another Daimler 1st speed gone – Correct tempers of these gears doubtful.	
	20/12/15		Daily Inspection – Difficulty in procuring Daimler gears from Advanced M.T. Depot – Have experimental set running for some weeks with tempers of gears considerably lowered – appears to be going strong. Must allow air for re-examination after return from leave. In the hands of rather a rough driver. So were getting a good test.	
	21/12/15		Daily Inspection – Battho set – Fitting Electric light to all cars	
	22/12/15		do.	do.

Army Form C. 2118

WAR DIARY
or
INTELLIGENCE SUMMARY

(Erase heading not required.)

Instructions regarding War Diaries and Intelligence Summaries are contained in F. S. Regs., Part II. and the Staff Manual respectively. Title Pages will be prepared in manuscript.

Place	Date	Hour	Summary of Events and Information	Remarks and references to Appendices
LA MENEGATE	23/12/15		Daily inspection. Fitting front electric lights to seven cars, expected to finish as quickly as possible.	
	24/12/15		Daily Inspection. Working late finishing electric lamps on cars.	
	25/12/15		Xmas day - daily inspection - afternoon sports with men.	
	26/12/15		Daily inspection M.S.I. O/C on leave at 5.40 a.m.	
	27/12/15		O/c on leave.	
	28/12/15		do	
	29/12/15		do Few minor repairs only - one bent front axle	
	30/12/15		do 2 Inverted lamps	
	31/12/15		do	

J Bayley
LIEUT, A.S.C.
COMMANDING 23rd DIV. F.A. & W.U.

1875 Wt. W593/826 1,000,000 4/15 J.B.C. & A. A.D.S.S./Forms/C. 2118.

238a ‡ A.W.U.
Vol.5-

F

January 1916

Army Form C. 2118

WAR DIARY
or
INTELLIGENCE SUMMARY

(Erase heading not required.)

Instructions regarding War Diaries and Intelligence Summaries are contained in F.S. Regs., Part II. and the Staff Manual respectively. Title Pages will be prepared in manuscript.

Place	Date	Hour	Summary of Events and Information	Remarks and references to Appendices
LA MENEGATE	1/1/16		O/c on leave	
	2/1/16		do	
	3/1/16		O/c returned from leave	
	4/1/16		Daily inspection — rain on types very great during last week	
	5/1/16		do minor repairs	
	6/1/16		do do	
	7/1/16		do do was very bad	
	8/1/16		do weather slightly improving	
	9/1/16		do do	
	10/1/16		do	
	11/1/16		do raining this evening	
	12/1/16		do First speed of Daimler beginning to give trouble	
	13/1/16		do All cars being reported thoroughly	

1875 Wt. W593/826 1,000,000 4/15 J.B.C. & A. A.D.S.S./Forms/C. 2118.

Confidential

War Diary
— of —
23rd Div. Field Ambulance & Workshop Unit

From 1st to 31st January 1916

P. Bayley ?
LIEUT, A.S.C.
COMMANDING 23RD DIV. F.A. & W.U.

Army Form C. 2118

WAR DIARY
or
INTELLIGENCE SUMMARY
(Erase heading not required.)

Place	Date	Hour	Summary of Events and Information	Remarks and references to Appendices
LA MENEGATE	14/16			
	15/16		Daily inspection — weather improving somewhat. but roads very bad. Lower part of road giving me approach to this farm is now impassable to cars.	
			Inspection: — Another front sheeve of Saunders going "quint" owing to attaining revergence — It would appear that the steel of which these gears are made is not up to the work. Any sudden additional strain be experienced — the inevitable result is that the trunnions of the cam immediately strips several teeth — these break off very short, quickly cause serious damage to the other gear which "ball races". —	
	16/16		Daily inspection — weather fine.	
	17/16		Daily inspection. — Another Saunders 1"speed gone". — It is to be hopes that the new type gears which are being supplied are complete set when any one gear gets type goes any. will	

WAR DIARY or INTELLIGENCE SUMMARY

Army Form C. 2118

Place	Date	Hour	Summary of Events and Information	Remarks and references to Appendices
LAMMENEGATE	18/1/16		Prior to be of better material & more capable of the harm work involved:—	
	19/1/16		Daily inspection — First two gear wheels of new sets arrived! First set forwarded on 7th Dec last — Have now seven cars on the road running without a first speed — necessitating very great care in handling. The delay in obtaining new sets which hon'y I gather, have been delivered upon since July 1915, would seem inexplicable. The car has de Clubet having to a braking gear wheel doing damage to other gears & to a certain ball race. Daily inspection:— weather fair	
	20/1/16		do do	
	21/1/16		do do	
	22/1/16		do weather fair — road entering farm very bad. Trainer Totching & draining. Meaning it will be difficult to move motor lorries when thaw comes to shift.	

Army Form C. 2118

WAR DIARY
or
INTELLIGENCE SUMMARY
(Erase heading not required.)

Instructions regarding War Diaries and Intelligence Summaries are contained in F.S. Regs., Part II. and the Staff Manual respectively. Title Pages will be prepared in manuscript.

Place	Date	Hour	Summary of Events and Information	Remarks and references to Appendices
LA NEUVEGATE	23/1/16		Another Daimler 1st speed gone:- Eight Cars now so running:- Weather improving	
	24/1/16		Daily inspection - minor repairs & renew to cars:-	
	25/1/16		Daily inspection. Still another Daimler 1st speed gone:- The gear wheels have every appearance of being made too hard, of poor quality steel:- The teeth invariably snap off very short. Nine cars now:-	
	26/1/16		Daily inspection - Three motor cycles out of running owing to inability to obtain wheel covers. Am addresses number to be obtained from England. Am endeavouring to obtain a suitable deal to make them myself.	
	27/1/16		Daily inspection - weather fair:-	
	28/1/16		do:- do:-	
	29/1/16		do:- Instruction to alter interior of all Ford Ambulances as per plan:- Shields have been built differently in front instances but they still come not with old type bodies:-	
	30/1/16		Daily inspection. Very misty & foggy:-	
	31/1/16		do:- Brendan Cahill Minor repairs A.D.S.S./C.&A.	

WAR DIARY
or
INTELLIGENCE SUMMARY

(Erase heading not required.)

Army Form C. 2118

Instructions regarding War Diaries and Intelligence Summaries are contained in F.S. Regs., Part II. and the Staff Manual respectively. Title Pages will be prepared in manuscript.

Place	Date	Hour	Summary of Events and Information	Remarks and references to Appendices
LA MERGATE	31/1/16		The leading feature of the Month has been the appalling wear on tyres of ambulance cars - due to the fact that the very bad condition of the roads can only be dealt with by spreading loose flints & filling up holes with similar materials - Running in mud the poor foundations of the roads in the first instance it is surprising that we are able to keep them even in any sort of condition for use :- Strong protests as to absolute necessity of provision of new & it is to be hoped more suitable gears for Daimler cars have brought forth a promise of ready supply - but & motorcycles running parts we still unprocurable :-	

P Bayley, LIEUT, A.S.C.
COMMANDING 23RD DIV. F.A. & W.U.

WAR DIARIES

of

23rd Divisional Field Ambulance Workshop Unit, A.S.C.

For the months of February and March 1916

23 FA.W.V.
Vol 6

Confidential

War Diary

of

23rd Div. F.A. & W.U.

from 1st Febry. to 29 Febry. 1916.

J Bayley
LIEUT, A.S.C.
COMMANDING 23RD DIV. F.A. & S.S.

Army Form C. 2118

Instructions regarding War Diaries and Intelligence Summaries are contained in F.S. Regs., Part II. and the Staff Manual respectively. Title Pages will be prepared in manuscript.

WAR DIARY
or
INTELLIGENCE SUMMARY
(Erase heading not required.)

Particulars

Place	Date	Hour	Summary of Events and Information	Remarks and references to Appendices
LA MENEGATE	1/16		Daily Inspection	
	2/16		do	
	3/16		do. Tried to evacuate No. hol I cylinder, apparently impossible to procure wheel bearings for same - my machine guns all right with this exception - Apparently these Spare parts are kept back at base repair shops :-	
	4/16		Reg. Inspection	
	5/16		do.	
	6/16		do.	
	7/16		do. One Daimler back also + gear box collapsed, which I attribute to the fact that car is running without a bottom speed - Differential pinions + bevels broken up. Receiving pleads of 2nd + 3rd + top gears for Daimlery	
	8/16		By Inspection - Tried no final speed and countershaft - "out of stock". It would	

1875. Wt. W593/826 1,000,000 4/15 J.B.C. & A. A.D.S.S./Forms/C. 2118.

Army Form C. 2118

WAR DIARY
or
INTELLIGENCE SUMMARY
(Erase heading not required.)

Instructions regarding War Diaries and Intelligence Summaries are contained in F. S. Regs, Part II. and the Staff Manual respectively. Title Pages will be prepared in manuscript.

Place	Date	Hour	Summary of Events and Information	Remarks and references to Appendices
LA MENEGATE	9/7/16		appear that they must be obtaining from makers in complete sets — otherwise a larger supply of tht gear which always goes first would be obtainable. Am informed officially that a new type of Daimler gears "Air hardened" — is being used in Renegeat lorries. (a further corroboration of the experience as to the defective nature of present gears — It would be desirable if the gear box itself could be redesigned & made more accessible — so that it were not necessary to take the chassis practically to pieces before a new gear can be inserted.	
	10/7/16		By inspection — another Daimler back axle collapsed — differential pinion & bevels smashed up, breaking differential casing itself — apparently for same reason — no fault speed.	
	11/7/16		By inspection	
	12/7/16		do.	

Army Form C. 2118

WAR DIARY
or
INTELLIGENCE SUMMARY
(Erase heading not required.)

Instructions regarding War Diaries and Intelligence Summaries are contained in F. S. Regs., Part II. and the Staff Manual respectively. Title Pages will be prepared in manuscript.

Place	Date	Hour	Summary of Events and Information	Remarks and references to Appendices
LAMOTTE(?)GATE	13/2/16		Sly inspection	
	14/2/16		Sly inspection. Lorries yet of Daimler 1st speed — As division is shortly moving into comparatively hilly country this is serious trouble is feared.	
	15/2/16		Sly inspection	
	16/2/16		do. Tyre wear getting very heavy	
	17/2/16		do. Lorries differential gears used for shall probably have to tour the Mr Daimlers out not with us.	
	18/2/16		Sly Inspection. Several sections of (?) Ambulances have moved away. Tyre wear abnormal — but never covers for day — have been forced to wire for further supplies as reserve seriously depleted.	
	19/2/16		Sly Inspection. Visited Mosbergue(?) — only to find that	

1875 Wt. W593/826 1,000,000 4/15 J.B.C. & A. A.D.S.S./Forms/C. 2118.

WAR DIARY
or
INTELLIGENCE SUMMARY

(Erase heading not required.)

Army Form C. 2118

Instructions regarding War Diaries and Intelligence Summaries are contained in F. S. Regs., Part II. and the Staff Manual respectively. Title Pages will be prepared in manuscript.

Place	Date	Hour	Summary of Events and Information	Remarks and references to Appendices
LAMENEGATE	20/7/16		Billet suggested as suitable for workshops by A.D.V.S. not available - being already occupied. Him motored to Wilk Mobecques again knowing endeavour to find accommodation at the Chateau with 70th F.A. Ambulance	
	21/7/16	4.30pm	Despatch rider in with news of Terror collision - quite near Mobecques (new station) send out breakdown gang to get car placed in proper hands until we move in 26/7/16 - whole car broken & not towable	
	21/7/16		Packing preparatory to moving early tomorrow	
MORBECQUES	22/7/16		Moving to Mobecques. Heavy snowstorm whole way - towing two cyclers with offside gale.	
	23/7/16		Much snow —	
	24/7/16		Still more snow	
	25/7/16		Improving weather	
	26/7/16		do do Very cold	

WAR DIARY
or
INTELLIGENCE SUMMARY

Army Form C. 2118

Place	Date	Hour	Summary of Events and Information	Remarks and references to Appendices
MONCHEQUES	27/7/16		Weather improving	
	28/7/16		Reports of a wet & damaged aeroplane being unable to obtain any news of its speed.	
	29/7/16		Orders to move with 70th F.A. at 9 a.m. received at 4 a.m. - Packed up at once & reported to O/C 70th F.A. at 6.50 a.m. F.A. not ready to move for two hours. Awaited my departure at once for BRUAY — Reached BRUAY at 1 p.m. Very difficult to find billets accommodation for horses &c.	

P. Barcley, LIEUT., A.S.C.
COMMANDING 23RD DIV. F.A. & N.U.

23 F.A.W.U.
Vol 7

Confidential.

War Diary

of

23rd Div. F. A. T.W.U.

from 1st — 31st March 1916

J.V. Bayley
LIEUT, A.S.C.
COMMANDING 23RD DIV. F.A. S. W.U.

Army Form C. 2118.

Instructions regarding War Diaries and Intelligence Summaries are contained in F.S. Regs., Part II. and the Staff Manual respectively. Title pages will be prepared in manuscript.

WAR DIARY
or
INTELLIGENCE SUMMARY.
(Erase heading not required.)

Place	Date	Hour	Summary of Events and Information	Remarks and references to Appendices
BRUAY	1 3/16		Binney:-	
	2 3/16		Instructions to hand over four old Daimler axles with defective gears received. Cars collected axles removed - Snowing hard.	
	3 3/16		6 axles despatched to No. 3 A.S.C. Repair Shop. Two more received in exchange - Still snowing - men working under difficulties from front 3 more old axles removed.	
	4 3/16		3 old Daimler axles exchanged.	
	5 3/16		Whole 9 new axles refitted & cars despatched by midday.	
	6 3/16		Snowy. Impediment. F.A. much scattered	
	7 3/16		do. Cars still worked	
	8 3/16		do	
	9 3/16		do	
	10 3/16		do	

Army Form C. 2118.

WAR DIARY
or
INTELLIGENCE SUMMARY.
(Erase heading not required.)

Instructions regarding War Diaries and Intelligence Summaries are contained in F. S. Regs., Part II. and the Staff Manual respectively. Title pages will be prepared in manuscript.

Place	Date	Hour	Summary of Events and Information	Remarks and references to Appendices
BRUAY	11/3/16		Instructions to move to GAUCHIN-LE-GAL. Packed & moved off at 9-30 - arrived 11.45 am - unpacked	
	12/3/16		12-30 instructions received that move cancelled - repacked & moved back to BRUAY same night	
	13/3/16		G.A. much accepted - difficult to inspect	
	14/3/16		The Armed Inspected & spare M.T. to B.Mr	
	15/3/16		Another defective Saunders axle exchanged. Saunders axle gone	
	16/3/16		daily inspection	
	17/3/16		do	
	18/3/16		do	
	19/3/16		do	
	20/3/16		Foden steamer inoperable. Very fair condition - certain joints (adrs. to) unobtainable from base - motorist by inspector to establish from Steam Co. Hazebrouck. Motorcyclist despatched therefor — None to be got & forced to make impromptu joints of asbestos string.	

Army Form C. 2118.

WAR DIARY
or
INTELLIGENCE SUMMARY.
(Erase heading not required.)

Instructions regarding War Diaries and Intelligence Summaries are contained in F. S. Regs., Part II. and the Staff Manual respectively. Title pages will be prepared in manuscript.

Place	Date	Hour	Summary of Events and Information	Remarks and references to Appendices
BRUAY	21/3/16		Daily inspection	
	22/3/16		do. – Moved to BARLIN to join 71st F.A.	
BARLIN	23/3/16		do	
	24/3/16		do	Very much weather
	25/3/16		do	do
	26/3/16		The old Sounders to be despatched & exchanged for new ones	
	27/3/16		New ones fitted. Daily inspection of all cars	
	28/3/16		Daily inspection	
	29/3/16		do	
	30/3/16		do	
	31/3/16		do – arranged with O/C 71 F.A. to keep an eye upon Workshop during my leave	

J. Bayley LIEUT, A.S.C.
COMMANDING 23rd DIV. F.A. & W.O.

T.134. Wt. W708–776. 500000. 4/15. Sir J. C. & S.

www.ingramcontent.com/pod-product-compliance
Lightning Source LLC
Chambersburg PA
CBHW081246170426
43191CB00037B/2055